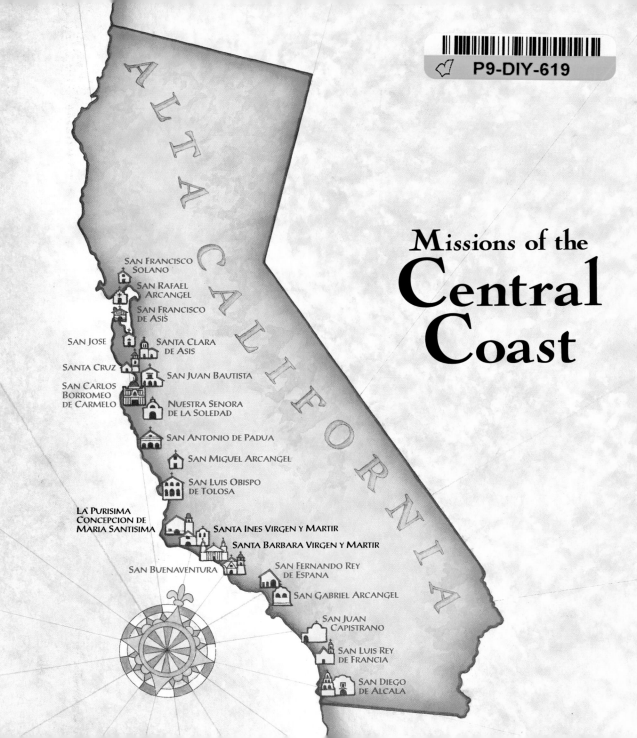

ALTA CALIFORNIA

Missions of the
# Central
# Coast

San Francisco Solano
San Rafael Arcangel
San Francisco de Asis
San Jose
Santa Clara de Asis
Santa Cruz
San Juan Bautista
San Carlos Borromeo de Carmelo
Nuestra Senora de la Soledad
San Antonio de Padua
San Miguel Arcangel
San Luis Obispo de Tolosa
La Purisima Concepcion de Maria Santisima
Santa Ines Virgen y Martir
Santa Barbara Virgen y Martir
San Buenaventura
San Fernando Rey de Espana
San Gabriel Arcangel
San Juan Capistrano
San Luis Rey de Francia
San Diego de Alcala

California
MISSIONS

# Missions of the
# Central
# Coast

*June Behrens*

LERNER PUBLICATIONS COMPANY

Series editors: Karen Chernyaev, Mary M. Rodgers, Elizabeth Verdick
Series photo researcher: Amy Cox
Series designer: Zachary Marell

*This book is available in two editions:*
Library binding by Lerner Publications Company
Soft cover by First Avenue Editions, 1999.
241 First Aveneue North
Minneapolis, MN 55401
ISBN: 0–8225–1930–5 (lib. bdg.)
ISBN: 0–8225–9832–9 (pbk.)

Website address: www.lernerbooks.com

LIBRARY OF CONGRESS CATALOGING-IN-PUBLICATION DATA

Behrens, June.
    Missions of the central coast / June Behrens.
      p.  cm. — (California missions)
    Includes index.
    Summary: Charts the histories of the California missions of Santa Bárbara, La Purísima Concepción, and Santa Inés, and briefly describes life among the Chumash Indians before the arrival of the Spaniards.
    ISBN 0–8225–1930–5 (lib. bdg.)
    1. Spanish mission buildings—California—Pacific Coast—Juvenile literature. 2. Pacific Coast (Calif.)—History, Local—Juvenile literature. 3. Pacific Coast (Calif.)—Church history—Juvenile literature. [1. Mission—California. 2. California—History. 3. Chumash Indians—Missions—California. 4. Indians of North America—Missions—California.]
    I. Title. II. Series.
    F862.B47 1995
    979.4'702—dc20                                                    95–2875

Manufactured in the United States of America
2 3 4 5 6 7 – JR – 03 02 01 00 99 98

*Cover:* **Sunlight bathes the arcade at Mission Santa Inés, the nineteenth settlement of the mission chain.** *Title page: Geometric artwork decorates the chapel at Santa Inés.*

To a new generation of Californios: Travis Hank Behrens and Lyndee Johnson

Every effort has been made to secure permission for the quoted material and for the photographs in this book.

# CONTENTS

# GLOSSARY

**adobe:** A type of clay soil found in Mexico and in dry parts of the United States. In Alta California, workers formed wet adobe into bricks that hardened in the sun.

**Alta California** (Upper California): An old Spanish name for the present-day state of California.

**Baja California** (Lower California): A strip of land off the northwestern coast of Mexico that lies between the Pacific Ocean and the Gulf of California. Part of Mexico, Baja California borders the U.S. state of California.

**Franciscan:** A member of the Order of Friars Minor, a Roman Catholic community founded in Italy by Saint Francis of Assisi in 1209. The Franciscans are dedicated to performing missionary work and acts of charity.

**mission:** A center where missionaries (religious teachers) work to spread their beliefs to other people and to teach a new way of life.

**missionary:** A person sent out by a religious group to spread its beliefs to other people.

**neophyte:** A Greek word meaning "newly converted" that refers to an Indian baptized into the Roman Catholic community.

**New Spain:** A large area once belonging to Spain that included what are now the southwestern United States and Mexico. After 1821, when New Spain had gained its independence from the Spanish Empire, the region became known as the Republic of Mexico.

**presidio:** A Spanish fort for housing soldiers. In Alta California, Spaniards built presidios to protect the missions and priests from possible attacks and to enforce order in the region. California's four main presidios were located at San Diego, Santa Barbara, Monterey, and San Francisco.

**quadrangle:** A four-sided enclosure surrounded by buildings.

**reservation:** Tracts of land set aside by the U.S. government to be used by Native Americans.

**secularization:** A series of laws enacted by the Mexican government in the 1830s. The rulings aimed to take mission land and buildings from Franciscan control and to place the churches in the hands of parish priests, who didn't perform missionary work. Much of the land was distributed to families and individuals.

# PRONUNCIATION GUIDE*

| | |
|---|---|
| Cabrillo, Juan Rodríguez | kah-BREE-yoh, WAHN roh-DREE-gays |
| Chumash | CHOO-mash |
| El Camino Reál | el kah-MEE-noh ray-AHL |
| La Purísima Concepción de Maria Santísima | lah poo-REE-see-mah con-thep-thee-OHN day mah-REE-ah sahn-TEE-see-mah |
| Lasuén, Fermín Francisco de | lah-soo-AYN, fair-MEEN frahn-SEES-koh day |
| Portolá, Gaspar de | por-toh-LAH, gahs-PAHR day |
| Pico, Pío | PEE-koh, PEE-oh |
| Sagimomatsse, Andrés | sah-hee-moh-MAHTZ, ahn-DRAYS |
| Santa Bárbara Virgen y Mártir | SAHN-tah BAHR-bahr-ah veer-HAYN ee MAHR-teer |
| Santa Inés Virgen y Mártir | SAHN-tah ee-NAYS veer-HAYN ee MAHR-teer |
| Serra, Junípero | SEH-rrah, hoo-NEE-pay-roh |
| Tápis, Estéban | TAH-pees, ehs-TAY-bahn |
| Vizcaíno, Sebastián | vees-kah-EE-noh, say-bahs-tee-AHN |

* Local pronunciations may differ.

# PREFACE

The religious beliefs and traditions of the Indians of California teach that the blessings of a rich land and a mild climate are gifts from the Creator. The Indians show their love and respect for the Creator—and for all of creation—by carefully managing the land for future generations and by living in harmony with the natural environment.

Over the course of many centuries, the Indians of California organized small, independent societies. Only in the hot, dry deserts of southeastern California did they farm the land to feed themselves. Elsewhere, the abundance of fish, deer, antelope, waterfowl, and wild seeds supplied all that the Indians needed for survival. The economies of these societies did not create huge surpluses of food. Instead the people produced only what they expected would meet their needs. Yet there is no record of famine during the long period when Indians in California managed the land.

These age-old beliefs and practices stood in sharp contrast to the policies of the Spaniards who began to settle areas of California in the late 1700s. Spain established religious missions along the coast to anchor its empire in California. At these missions, Spanish priests baptized thousands of Indians into the Roman Catholic religion. Instead of continuing to hunt and gather their food, the Indians were made to work on mission estates where farming supported the settlements. Pastures for mission livestock soon took over Indian land, and European farming activities depleted native plants. Illnesses that the Spaniards had unintentionally carried from Europe brought additional suffering to many Indian groups.

The Indians living in California numbered 340,000 in the late 1700s, but only 100,000 remained after roughly 70 years of Spanish missionization. Many of the Indians died from disease. Spanish soldiers killed other Indians during native revolts at the missions. Some entire Indian societies were wiped out.

Thousands of mission Indian descendants proudly continue to practice their native culture and to speak their native language. But what is most important to these survivors is that their people's history be understood by those who now call California home, as well as by others across the nation. Through this series of books, young readers will learn for the first time how the missions affected the Indians and their traditional societies.

Perhaps one of the key lessons to be learned from an honest and evenhanded account of California's missions is that the Indians had something important to teach the Spaniards and the people who came to the region later. Our ancestors and today's elders instill in us that we must respect and live in harmony with animals, plants, and one another. While this is an ancient wisdom, it seems especially relevant to our future survival.

*Professor Edward D. Castillo*
Cahuilla-Luiseño Mission Indian Descendant

# INTRODUCTION

FOUNDED BY SPAIN, THE CALIFORNIA **MISSIONS** ARE located on a narrow strip of California's Pacific coast. Some of the historic buildings sit near present-day Highway 101, which roughly follows what was once a roadway called El Camino Reál (the Royal Road), so named to honor the king of Spain. The trail linked a chain of 21 missions set up between 1769 and 1823.

Spain, along with leaders of the Roman Catholic Church, established missions and *presidios* (forts) throughout the Spanish Empire to strengthen its claim to the land. In the 1600s, Spain built mission settlements on the peninsula known as **Baja California,** as well as in other areas of **New Spain** (present-day Mexico).

The goal of the Spanish mission system in North America was to make Indians accept Spanish ways and become loyal subjects of the Spanish king. Priests functioning as **missionaries** (religious teachers) tried to convert the local Indian populations to Catholicism and to

*In the mid-1700s, Native Americans living in what is now California came into contact with Roman Catholic missionaries from Spain.*

11

*The grounds of Mission Santa Bárbara hold a statue of a Chumash Indian. The Chumash were the main Native American group recruited to the missions of the central coast.*

teach them to dress and behave like Spaniards. Soldiers came to protect the missionaries and to make sure the Indians obeyed the priests.

During the late 1700s, Spain wanted to spread its authority northward from Baja California into the region known as **Alta California,** where Spain's settlement pattern would be repeated. The first group of Spanish soldiers and missionaries traveled to Alta California in 1769. The missionaries, priests of the **Franciscan** order, were led by Junípero Serra, the father-president of the mission system.

The soldiers and missionaries came into contact with communities of Native Americans, or Indians, that dotted the coastal and inland areas of Alta California. For thousands of years, the region had been home to many Native American groups that spoke a wide variety of languages. Using these Indians as unpaid laborers was vital to the success of the mission system. The mission economy was based on agriculture—a way of life unfamiliar to local Indians, who mostly hunted game and gathered wild plants for food.

Although some Indians willingly joined the missions, the Franciscans relied on various methods to convince or force other Native Americans to become part of the mission system. The priests sometimes lured Indians with gifts of glass beads and colored cloth or other items new to the Native Americans. Some Indians who lost their hunting and food-gathering grounds to mission farms and ranches joined the Spanish settlements to survive. In other cases, Spanish soldiers forcibly took villagers from their homes.

**Neophytes,** or Indians recruited into the missions, were expected to learn the Catholic faith and the skills for farming and building. Afterward—Spain reasoned—the Native Americans would be able to manage the property themselves, a process that officials figured would take 10 years. But a much different turn of events took place.

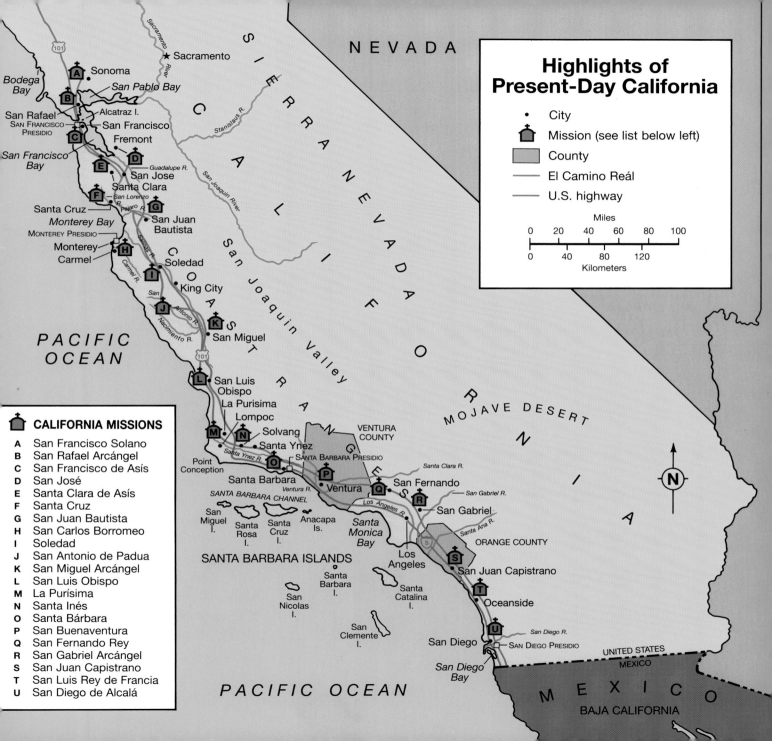

# Highlights of Present-Day California

- • City
-  Mission (see list below left)
- County
- El Camino Reál
- U.S. highway

Miles
0  20  40  60  80  100

0  40  80  120
Kilometers

NEVADA

SIERRA NEVADA

CALIFORNIA

COAST RANGES

MOJAVE DESERT

PACIFIC OCEAN

UNITED STATES
MEXICO

MEXICO
BAJA CALIFORNIA

## CALIFORNIA MISSIONS

| | |
|---|---|
| A | San Francisco Solano |
| B | San Rafael Arcángel |
| C | San Francisco de Asís |
| D | San José |
| E | Santa Clara de Asís |
| F | Santa Cruz |
| G | San Juan Bautista |
| H | San Carlos Borromeo |
| I | Soledad |
| J | San Antonio de Padua |
| K | San Miguel Arcángel |
| L | San Luis Obispo |
| M | La Purísima |
| N | Santa Inés |
| O | Santa Bárbara |
| P | San Buenaventura |
| Q | San Fernando Rey |
| R | San Gabriel Arcángel |
| S | San Juan Capistrano |
| T | San Luis Rey de Francia |
| U | San Diego de Alcalá |

Sacramento River

Bodega Bay
Sonoma
San Pablo Bay
San Rafael
SAN FRANCISCO PRESIDIO
Alcatraz I.
San Francisco
San Francisco Bay
Fremont
Guadalupe R.
Santa Clara
San Jose
San Lorenzo R.
Pajaro R.
Santa Cruz
Monterey Bay
MONTEREY PRESIDIO
Monterey
Carmel
Carmel R.
Salinas R.
Soledad
King City
San Antonio R.
Nacimiento R.
San Miguel
San Luis Obispo
La Purisima
Lompoc
Solvang
Santa Ynez
Santa Ynez R.
SANTA BARBARA PRESIDIO
Point Conception
Santa Barbara
Ventura R.
Ventura
VENTURA COUNTY
Santa Clara R.
San Fernando
San Gabriel R.
San Gabriel
Santa Ana R.
ORANGE COUNTY
San Juan Capistrano
Oceanside
Los Angeles R.
Santa Monica Bay
Los Angeles
San Diego R.
San Diego
SAN DIEGO PRESIDIO
San Diego Bay

SANTA BARBARA CHANNEL
San Miguel I.
Santa Rosa I.
Santa Cruz I.
Anacapa Is.
SANTA BARBARA ISLANDS
Santa Barbara I.
San Nicolas I.
Santa Catalina I.
San Clemente I.

Stanislaus R.
San Joaquin River
San Joaquin Valley

PACIFIC OCEAN

| California Mission | Founding Date |
|---|---|
| San Diego de Alcalá | July 16, 1769 |
| San Carlos Borromeo de Carmelo | June 3, 1770 |
| San Antonio de Padua | July 14, 1771 |
| San Gabriel Arcángel | September 8, 1771 |
| San Luis Obispo de Tolosa | September 1, 1772 |
| San Francisco de Asís | June 29, 1776 |
| San Juan Capistrano | November 1, 1776 |
| Santa Clara de Asís | January 12, 1777 |
| San Buenaventura | March 31, 1782 |
| Santa Bárbara Virgen y Mártir | December 4, 1786 |
| La Purísima Concepción de Maria Santísima | December 8, 1787 |
| Santa Cruz | August 28, 1791 |
| Nuestra Señora de la Soledad | October 9, 1791 |
| San José | June 11, 1797 |
| San Juan Bautista | June 24, 1797 |
| San Miguel Arcángel | July 25, 1797 |
| San Fernando Rey de España | September 8, 1797 |
| San Luis Rey de Francia | June 13, 1798 |
| Santa Inés Virgen y Mártir | September 17, 1804 |
| San Rafael Arcángel | December 14, 1817 |
| San Francisco Solano | July 4, 1823 |

Forced to give up their age-old traditions, many Native Americans didn't adjust to mission life. In fact, most Indians died soon after entering the missions—mainly from European diseases that eventually killed thousands of Indians throughout California.

Because hundreds of Indian laborers worked at each mission, most of the settlements thrived. The missions produced grapes, olives, wheat, cattle hides, cloth, soap, candles, and other goods. In fact, the missions successfully introduced to Alta California a variety of crops and livestock that still benefit present-day Californians.

The missions became so productive that the Franciscans established a valuable trade network. Mission priests exchanged goods and provided nearby soldiers and settlers with provisions. The agricultural wealth of the missions angered many settlers and soldiers, who resented

*On lands that once were part of Mission Santa Bárbara, farmers grow Bibb lettuce. The Franciscan priests who ran the missions in the 1700s and 1800s introduced many crops to the region.*

the priests for holding Alta California's most fertile land and the majority of the livestock and for controlling the Indian labor force.

This resentment grew stronger after 1821, when New Spain became the independent country of Mexico. Mexico claimed Alta California and began the **secularization** of the missions. The mission churches still offered religious services, but the Spanish Franciscans were to be replaced by secular priests. These priests weren't missionaries seeking to convert people.

By 1836 the neophytes were free to leave the missions, and the settlements quickly declined from the loss of workers. Few of the former neophytes found success away from the missions, however. Many continued as laborers on *ranchos* (ranches) or in nearby *pueblos* (towns), earning little or no pay.

In 1848 Mexico lost a war against the United States and ceded Alta California to the U.S. government. By that time, about half of Alta California's Indian population had died. Neophytes who had remained at the missions often had no village to which to return. They moved to pueblos or to inland areas. Meanwhile, the missions went into a state of decay, only to be rebuilt years later.

This book will focus on three missions that line the central coast of California. Mission Santa Bárbara Virgen y Mártir, the tenth settlement in the chain, was founded in 1786. A year later, missionaries set up La Purísima Concepción de Maria Santísima as the eleventh mission. One of the last missions to be established, Santa Inés Virgen y Mártir dates to 1804 and sits between Santa Bárbara and La Purísima in the Santa Ynez Valley.

*Series Editors*

# PART ONE

# *Early Life along the Coast*

HUGE OCEAN WAVES CRASHED ON THE SANDY BEACH. The people heard the pounding of the surf and the calls of seabirds. Gulls landed onshore near tide pools and salt marshes, where men and women gathered shellfish. Clams, mollusks, and abalones were part of their diet. Sometimes the people watched playful dolphins leap in the nearby channel. Whales, too, occasionally rose for air, then dove deep beneath the sea.

The people of the coastal region were Chumash Indians. For thousands of years, they and their ancestors called this land home. Large Chumash villages covered the sunlit shore and inland areas. Across

*Waves from the Pacific Ocean beat against the cliffs of the central coast, where seaweed and shellfish (bottom inset) provide food for circling gulls (top inset).*

*Once home to Chumash Indians, San Miguel Island (above left) now hosts elephant seals and other sea life. Mainland Chumash built their villages near water sources, such as the Santa Ynez River (above). Oak trees (below left), from which the Native Americans gathered acorns (inset), dotted Chumash territory.*

the Pacific Ocean, against the blue horizon, stood a chain of offshore islands where many other Chumash lived.

On the mainland, the rugged sea cliffs were sometimes shrouded in fog. Low, rolling hills rose beyond the shore. Farther inland the Santa Ynez River watered grassy valleys. Oak, maple, and sycamore trees grew along the riverbanks. Far in the distance lay rugged mountains. Beyond them were dry plains and desert.

The Chumash felt fortunate that their territory was warm most of the year. The land provided for their needs. Oak trees, for example, supplied the acorn, a nut that Chumash women ground up to make a mushlike food staple. The ocean brought forth fish, sea mammals, and seaweed. A variety of native plants, also gathered by the women, were a source of medicine as well as food. The people and the land were in harmony.

**Selected Native American Groups in Central and Southern California around 1500**

Pomo
Patwin
Lake Miwok
Wappo
Nisenan
Coast Miwok
Miwok
Ohlone
Northern Valley Yokuts
Foothill Yokuts
Esselen
Monache
Salinan
Southern Valley Yokuts
Tubatulabal
Kitanemuk
Tataviam
Chumash
Serrano
Chumash
Tongva
Tongva (Gabrielino, Fernandeño)
Shoshonean-Speakers (Luiseño, Cahuilla, Acagchemem)
Yuman-Speakers (Diegueño, Kumeyaay)

N

## Daily Life

About 200 years ago, roughly 15,000 Chumash were living in the central coast region of what is now California. Each community housed a few hundred people and bustled with the sounds of daily life.

At dawn people rose to start the day. Dogs and children scampered noisily. Women, dressed in buckskin skirts, pounded acorns on stone slabs or gathered grasses for basket weaving. Meanwhile, the women kept an eye on their babies and other children. Youngsters learned the chores and customs of their village by watching the adults.

Men split wooden planks to build *tomols* (canoes) that were up to 20 feet long. The Chumash used these vessels for fishing and for carrying as many as 10 people to and from the islands. Wearing a belt that held their hunting weapons, the men shot small game with bows and

(*Above*) *A typical Chumash village included many grass-covered dwellings. The long plank canoes, called* tomols, *were used for both fishing and transportation.* (*Below*) **In Chumash villages, women and girls did most of the food preparation and cooking, including grinding acorns into flour.**

# A Chumash Story

When darkness fell, villagers gathered around the old storyteller and grew quiet. The elder, in a hushed voice, began his tale of how their people had come to be.

Snilemun ("Coyote of the Sky") and Slǒw ("Great Eagle Who Knows What Is to Be") talked about how they would make human beings. Snilemun announced that people should look like him and have his fine hands. Slǒw disagreed at first but finally gave in. Lizard, who stood nearby, listened to them in silence night after night.

Then the three creatures gathered around a smooth, white rock. Anything that touched the stone would leave a mark. Just as Snilemun was about to stamp his hand in the rock, quiet Lizard reached out and quickly pressed his own handprint onto the flat surface. Before anyone could stop him, Lizard escaped into a deep crevice among the rocks.

That is how the people got their hands. "I am finished," the storyteller said, "it is the end."

arrows and took geese and ducks from lagoons. Before the sun went down, fishermen beached their tomols and hauled ashore their catch of shark, bass, or bonito.

Chumash villages had many different buildings. Families put up dome-shaped homes using poles made from young willow trees. After the poles had been secured to the ground, they were bent into an arch. The frame was then covered with strong, coarse grasses that had been woven together.

The Indians used some structures to store dried foods for the winter months. Other buildings included the *temescal,* or sweat lodge. In these heated structures, men gathered to purify their bodies before a hunt or a ceremony.

Most villages had an area set aside for games and ceremonial dances. Women played games of chance, using dice fashioned from walnut shells filled with tar. Gambling sticks made of split wood were tossed to see whether the flattened side fell up or down. Many Chumash enjoyed hoop and pole, a contest to see who could throw a long pole through a rolling hoop.

Dances, ceremonies, and celebrations took place on level ground in the village. Wrapped in a skirt of downy eagle feathers, shamans (religious leaders) performed village rituals. Some shamans, it was said, had the power to control the weather or to change into an animal. Shamans also acted as healers, using herbs and medicines to cure illnesses.

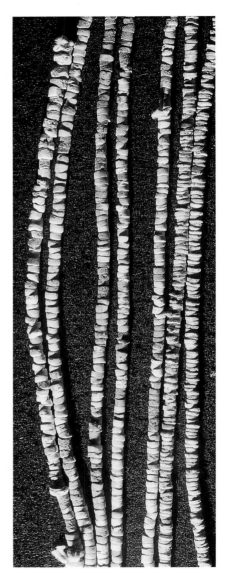

*The Chumash began to make rock paintings (below) about 1,000 years ago. The artworks feature human and animal figures and are thought to have religious meaning. Native American craftspeople produced necklaces (right) of shell or other natural materials.*

*An illustration from the 1800s shows Chumash dancing in celebration. The Indians used dance as a way of expressing thanks.*

Each village had one or more chiefs, who took charge of food supplies, shell-bead money, and other valuables. The coastal chiefs, who managed trade between inland and island peoples, held the most power. Chumash on the mainland exchanged many goods with neighboring peoples, using a network of trails that reached coastal and inland communities.

The Chumash scooped up shells to use as money. The Indians ground the shells into round, flat shapes before stringing them onto cords. The money's worth depended on the length of the cord and on the number of shells used.

Artisans in the villages made shell jewelry, oak bowls, and reed baskets. Their finely worked, sturdy baskets had many uses. Women carried babies in cradle-shaped baskets. Other types stored water and valuables. Some containers were made for plant foods, such as wild cherries, pine nuts, and mushrooms. The variety and abundance of fish, animals, plants, and other resources in the region kept the people well fed throughout the year.

The Chumash gave thanks to the earth for providing their communities with food and other necessities. To the Native Americans, the earth and sun—both givers of life—were sacred and deserved honor. The people offered seeds or poles topped with feathers to these life forces and honored them through dance and celebration. For the Chumash, keeping harmony with nature and all its bounty guided every event of their lives, from birth to death.

In 1542 the Chumash sighted large ships in what is now the Santa Barbara Channel. The Indians paddled their tomols to meet the strangers, who were explorers from Spain. The Spaniards claimed the region for the king of Spain and continued on their journey.

## European Contact

In 1542 Chumash villagers watched as three huge ships with full sails moved through the nearby channel. The ships had been sent by King Charles I of Spain, who was interested in claiming the lands for his empire. The explorer Juan Rodríguez Cabrillo—the first European to land on the coast of what the Spaniards called Alta California—captained the vessels.

Cabrillo and his crew planned to chart the unfamiliar shores of the central coast. The Chumash from the region loaded gifts of food and other goods into their tomols and paddled out to meet the ships. The crew admired the fine crafting of the boats and the friendly nature of the people. The Indians provided a feast of bonito for the strangers. In exchange for food and fresh water, the Europeans gave the Native Americans glass beads and other objects. Cabrillo then simply claimed the land for Spain and sailed on.

Many years passed before the Chumash met Europeans again. In 1602 the Spanish ships of Sebastián Vizcaíno followed Cabrillo's route. Vizcaíno sailed into the channel and gave present-day Santa Barbara its name.

More than 100 years later, Spain began to establish permanent settlements, or missions, along the coast of Alta California. Spain's political goal was to keep foreigners away from its empire and to secure its claim to the land. At the mission outposts, Franciscans taught native peoples the Catholic faith. The goal of the Spanish missionaries was to turn the Indians into loyal Spanish citizens and Roman Catholics. Father-President Junípero Serra led the Franciscans in this project.

Spanish soldiers came to protect the new missions from outsiders and from possible Indian attacks. Captain Gaspar de Portolá commanded the troops. In 1769—after helping to establish the first Spanish mission in Alta California—Captain Portolá traveled northward. On the journey, Portolá and his soldiers passed many Chumash villages. The Spaniards were amazed by the region's large Indian population.

Father Serra was enthusiastic about spreading his faith among the Chumash of the central coast. He was convinced that the Indians, whose villages were strongly organized, would fit in well at the Franciscan settlements. The mission Serra

ONE MEMBER OF THE CABRILLO EXPEDITION KEPT A DIARY . . . AND WROTE, "THE INDIANS WERE VERY FRIENDLY. . . . THERE WERE MANY CANOES, FOR THE WHOLE COAST IS VERY DENSELY POPULATED . . . ."

wanted to establish would be named after Saint Barbara.

But, before Serra could set up this new mission, the governor of New Spain, Felipe de Neve, chose to build a presidio near the proposed mission site. This guarded fort could protect the mission and Spanish settlers from foreigners and non-mission Indians. The governor told Father Serra that a mission couldn't be founded until after the presidio had been completed. Soldiers began building the fort and barracks in 1782.

Father Serra, who died in 1784, didn't live long enough to see the construction of Mission Santa Bárbara. Father Fermín Francisco de Lasuén became the new father-president. He chose a location that overlooked the ocean, the presidio, and a rich valley dotted with oak trees.

On December 4, 1786, Father Lasuén raised a cross and blessed the place now called Rocky Mound. This date marked the original founding of Mission Santa Bárbara, the tenth California mission. The official founding came 12 days later, when the new governor, Pedro Fages, arrived from New Spain to attend the ceremonies.

# PART TWO

# *Missions of the Central Coast*

MISSIONS SANTA BÁRBARA, LA PURÍSIMA, AND SANTA Inés share a common history. Protected by the presidio at Santa Barbara, the central coast missions were built amid large numbers of Chumash villages. The priests at the missions wanted to convert the local Chumash to the Catholic religion and to teach them Spanish ways. Eventually, the missionaries believed the Indians would be able to govern the missions as Spanish communities.

Many Chumash weren't interested in mission life and held fast to their own traditions for many years after the arrival of the Spaniards.

*Flowers bloom in front of Mission Santa Bárbara, the tenth mission in the chain. The settlement was named after Saint Barbara, an early convert to Christianity who was beheaded in Turkey in about A.D. 200.*

But in time—probably because of widespread drought that caused famine—Chumash families moved to the central coast missions. In so doing, they lost touch with some of their old customs.

# Mission Santa Bárbara

The Spaniards had brought glass beads to trade with local Chumash in exchange for work at Mission Santa Bárbara. With beads as payment, the Chumash helped the missionaries build a temporary chapel and living quarters of logs and thatch. Mud and stone filled any gaps left in the walls and roofs. Bare earth served as the floors. These structures eventually took the shape of a **quadrangle,** or four-sided design with an open courtyard in the center.

*Workers marked the sheep and cattle of Mission Santa Bárbara with this brand.*

The Spaniards also provided the Chumash with tools such as knives and needles. The Indians found these items useful in their own villages and willingly worked in exchange for the metal goods. Many Chumash also sought blankets and clothing from the priests. The Franciscans gave these materials only to Indians who underwent baptism (a ritual that welcomes a newcomer into a religious community).

As a result, many local Chumash came to Mission Santa Bárbara for the baptismal ceremony. Because they didn't speak Spanish, however, the Indians probably didn't understand what this ritual meant. The priests considered the baptized Indians, called neophytes, to be Catholics and expected them to follow Catholic teachings.

During the early years of the mission's history, the Chumash continued their traditional ways. The Indians used the temescal and danced and celebrated as they always had. They left seeds and feathered poles in sacred places near their villages.

The Chumash were able to practice their age-old customs because most of the people, even after being baptized, remained in their own communities. Although the priests preferred that the neophytes live at the mission, few of the Indians were willing to leave their homes. To make baptism attractive to the Native Americans, the priests

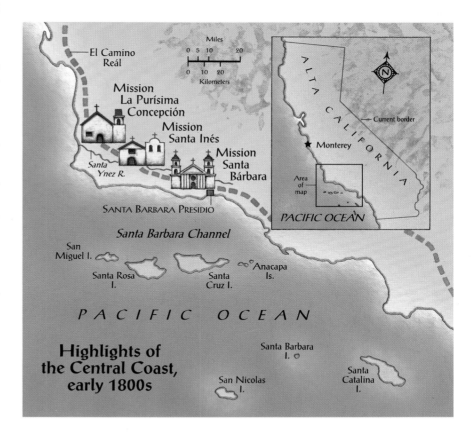

Highlights of the Central Coast, early 1800s

allowed many baptized Chumash to stay in their villages, where the priests had little control.

The Chumash, under the direction of the missionaries, improved the mission's buildings. Over time the Indians constructed a kitchen and storerooms. Many of the structures were made of **adobe,** a clay common to dry areas. The Indians formed adobe bricks from a combination of this clay, straw, and water.

The Indians quickly learned the techniques of building in the Spanish style. Skilled and hardworking, the Chumash enjoyed exploring new technologies. Workers mastered European farming methods by cutting down trees to create pastures for livestock and by planting and harvesting crops.

By 1787 the mission's buildings, fields, and pastures had taken up a lot of Chumash territory. Mission sheep and cattle grazed on land that, in the past, had provided the Chumash with a ready supply of seeds and plants. Crops and livestock had forced game animals from their habitats. In addition, a long drought caused further loss of native food resources. The mission, with its thriving fields and

*A modern painting gives a view of the area around Mission Santa Bárbara in the late 1700s.*

stable food supply, soon attracted many hungry Indian families.

## Mission Life

As more Chumash came to the mission, new structures went up along its quadrangle. The neophytes helped build three different adobe churches. Each structure was bigger and roomier than the one it replaced. Among other buildings were workshops, where neophytes learned a variety of trades such as blacksmithing and shoemaking. In other shops, neophyte women practiced European-style sewing and weaving. The women also made soap or candles using tallow (animal fat).

# The Coolest Water System

Mission Santa Bárbara's water system was extremely well engineered. It began with a creek that lay behind Santa Bárbara's lands. Chumash neophytes dammed the creek and built a network of sandstone-and-mortar walls called aqueducts. Running along the top of each aqueduct was a deep, narrow channel through which water from the dam could flow. The system's aqueducts eventually guided the water into a small reservoir

*Parts of the original aqueduct remain at Mission Santa Bárbara.*

(storage area). Then the water traveled in one of two directions—either straight to the mission to be used for drinking and cooking or into a much bigger reservoir. This larger container, which held up to 640,000 gallons, supplied the garden, the orchards, and an ornate fountain. Overflow from the fountain found its way into the mission's *lavandería* (laundry area), where neophyte women washed clothes.

*A full moon rises above one of the matching bell towers (left) of Santa Bárbara's church, which welcomed neophyte worshipers (below) in earlier times.*

Prayer and worship were important parts of daily life at the mission. The priests expected the Chumash to attend religious services every day. The ringing of the mission bells signaled when the Indians had to be at the church.

In 1801 the Indians at the mission were struck with illnesses that the Europeans had unknowingly brought to the region. Because the Chumash had never before been exposed to these sicknesses, many had no natural resistance and soon died. One of the victims at Mission Santa Bárbara was a shaman who had a vision. In her dream, she was told that all baptized Indians would die and that the only way to live would be to cancel each baptism using an Indian ritual.

Frightened Chumash from nearby villages and from the is- lands heard about the vision and arrived seeking the native cere- mony from the woman. As part of the ritual, neophytes at Santa Bárbara secretly built altars of sticks and thatch and presented gifts to native spirits. The priests soon discovered that the neo- phytes were practicing their tra- ditional religion openly and tried to end the activities.

A few years later, the Francis- cans became even more strict.

Officials in New Spain ordered priests to require neophytes to leave their villages and to live at the mission. Hundreds of neophytes reluctantly made the move.

From 1815 to 1820, work progressed on a fourth church at Mission Santa Bárbara—this one of stone. Historians believe that a master architect and stonemason from New Spain guided the project. He modeled the columned facade (front) of the church after an ancient European design. The beauty of the church at Santa Bárbara earned it the name "Queen of the Missions."

Father Antonio Ripoll, the priest in charge of Mission Santa Bárbara at the time, directed the neophyte workers. The laborers hauled sandstone to use as the building material for the church. They made curved red tiles of baked clay for the roof. An early French explorer named Eugène Duflot de Mofras remarked on the castlelike beauty of the mis-sion after sailing through the Santa Barbara Channel.

But some neophytes at the thriving mission weren't happy. The priests wanted the Chumash to give up their old ways and to learn the Spanish language. The Franciscans also wanted the Indians to dress in European clothing and to pray often. Some Chumash disregarded Franciscan teachings and

*The facade (front) of Mission Santa Bárbara's church reflects an architectural style—known as neoclassical—that was popular in Europe from the sixteenth century onward. The Franciscans referred to a book in the mission's library for details on how to construct a neoclassical-style building.*

returned to their Native American traditions.

Other neophytes fled the settlement to escape the routine of mission life. In fact, of all the California missions, Santa Bárbara had the most runaways. Soldiers caught many escaped Indians and brought them back to the mission for a whipping or other punishment.

To make mission life more appealing, the priests allowed the Indians to invite friends and family members to visit. The visitors often encouraged the neophytes to practice the old ways. For this reason, parts of Chumash culture stayed alive, no matter how hard the priests tried to end it.

## Rebellion

On February 21, 1824, a major Indian revolt began in the central coast region. The uprising started at nearby Mission Santa Inés, spread to La Purísima, and eventually engulfed Santa Bárbara as well.

At Mission Santa Bárbara, the *alcalde* (Indian manager of the neophytes) was Andrés Sagimomatsse. He received word that a revolt had broken out at Mission Santa Inés. Sagimomatsse sent the women and children of Santa Bárbara into the foothills for safety. The alcalde and several followers then secretly armed themselves and confronted Spanish soldiers at the mission. In the skirmish, four soldiers received minor wounds, while three Indians died and two were hurt.

Sagimomatsse then made plans to find other Native American groups who would be willing to launch a large-scale revolt against the non-native peoples. Unable to organize the raiders, the alcalde and his followers remained hidden for many weeks.

Spanish schoolboys were taught to develop a unique set of lines and curls to go with their signatures. The decoration, called a rubric, was hard to copy and set apart each signature. In fact, the rubric was more legally binding than the signature alone. Each Spanish-born priest in the mission system signed important papers with this distinctive drawing.

*Within sight of Mission Santa Bárbara, Spanish soldiers battled Chumash neophytes during the revolt of 1824.*

Living in the hills, the escaped Chumash gave up the teachings of the missionaries. The Indians didn't repeat Christian prayers, and they once again took up gambling, which had been forbidden at the mission. They said they would live in the "open country... [as] soldiers, stonemasons, [and] carpenters... [and] provide for ourselves by our work...." Many, however, ended up returning to the mission.

The 1824 revolt was probably the result of many frustrations shared by the Chumash of the central coast missions. The people were angry, for example, that the missions had taken up land the Indians had always counted on for survival. In the opinion of many Chumash, the Spaniards had brought sickness and death to Indians. Many Indians also disliked mission life and resented the harsh treatment of the soldiers. Unwilling to watch their culture and communities die out, the Chumash rebelled to survive.

# Mission La Purísima Concepción

A little more than a year after setting up Mission Santa Bárbara, Father Lasuén founded the eleventh mission in the chain—La Purísima Concepción de Maria Santísima—on December 8, 1787. The mission's name translates as "the Immaculate Conception of Mary the Most Pure." The site lay in a fertile valley near numerous Chumash villages.

Because the founding came during the rainy season, the Spaniards waited until the following spring to construct mission buildings. In March 1788, workers from Mission Santa Bárbara arrived to put up temporary structures. Within the next few months, the priests in charge of the mission baptized about 75 Chumash.

The Chumash came to the new mission for a variety of reasons. Some were curious. Others desired food or goods. Because of language barriers, however, the priests had a hard time explaining to the Native Americans what becoming part of the mission meant. Many Indians didn't realize that, in joining La Purísima, they would have to abandon their old religion.

*The flourishing herds of Mission La Purísima Concepción carried this brand. The mission was named after Mary, the mother of Jesus.*

La Purísima's church was completed around 1802. The Chumash also set up housing, workshops, and storerooms of adobe and clay tiles. The Indians planted fields of grain and helped to build canals to carry water to crops. Large herds of mission cattle grazed on nearby pastures. By 1804 more than 1,500 people were living at this flourishing mission.

In that year, Father Mariano Payeras arrived to run the settlement. He stayed at La Purísima for the next 19 years. At first the mission prospered under his direction. It pastured more than 20,000 head of livestock and produced a steady supply of hides, soap, candles, and wool. But disaster and hardship hampered the mission's ongoing success.

## Disaster Strikes

In December of 1812, a major earthquake rocked the mission. Giant cracks opened in the ground near the site. Heavy rains fell for days, and a wall of water poured down the slopes of nearby hills. The floods and a

*"THE EARTHQUAKE ENTIRELY DESTROYED THE CHURCH . . . , BURIED . . . THE VARIOUS IMAGES AND PAINTINGS, AND RUINED THE GREATER PART OF THE FURNITURE . . . . THE VERY HEAVY RAINFALLS THAT FOLLOWED PREVENT DIGGING OUT ANYTHING."*

season of rain that followed destroyed the mission buildings.

The priests and neophytes had no choice but to abandon La Purísima. In 1813 the Franciscans found a new spot for the mission across the Santa Ynez River. Father Payeras directed the construction of the new buildings.

Instead of following the usual quadrangle design, the new church and other structures stood in rows. This layout would allow people to escape more quickly in case of another disaster. Workers fashioned sturdy walls more than four feet thick and strengthened them with stone. The new mission featured a blacksmith shop, a weaving room, storehouses, and new vats for holding soap and tallow.

After the rebuilding, La Purísima thrived once again for a short period before being struck not by too much water but by too little. From 1816 to 1818, a severe drought dried out the land. Crops withered from lack of rain. Hundreds of sheep died of starvation. Then a fire in 1818 destroyed most of the neophyte housing.

After an earthquake leveled La Purísima, neophytes rebuilt the mission at a different site in rows *(above left)*—the only such layout in the mission chain. The successful settlement included a weaving room *(left)* and was known for its high-quality cattle hides *(above)*.

*A carreta, or wooden oxcart, was a common means of transporting goods and people in mission times.*

Outbreaks of smallpox and measles had often hit La Purísima, causing many neophytes to become ill and die. Around 1816 workers built an adobe hospital at the mission. At the hospital, Guadalupe Briones nursed the sick, using a combination of native and Spanish remedies, such as traditional herbs and teas. In spite of the care, few Chumash patients survived.

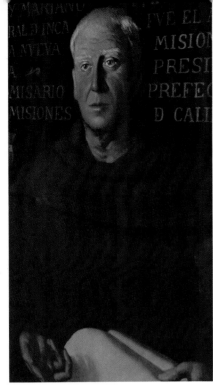

Within the next few years, the struggling mission received few supplies from the government. The neophytes had to work even harder to plant, harvest, and prepare food for the mission's population, for the nearby presidio, and for trade. In 1823 Father Payeras died, further weakening the mission.

*Father Mariano Payeras was the administrator of La Purísima for almost 20 years. He not only directed the Indian workforce but also guided the neophytes in spiritual matters. According to records, most Chumash who lived at the mission liked Father Payeras. Hubert Howe Bancroft, a U.S. historian who in the 1850s gathered materials about California's native peoples, wrote of him, "He was personally a popular man on account of his affable manners, kindness of heart, and unselfish devotion to the welfare of all."*

*In the early 1800s, neophytes at La Purísima worked hard to supply food and other necessities to the mission and the presidio.*

# Chumash Artists and Builders

Although the Franciscans were eager to teach the Chumash many skills from Europe, some of the priests also realized that the Indians had talents of their own. The Chumash were excellent craftspeople, for example, specializing in carving and sculpting. The Spaniards noted the fineness of Chumash stonework inlaid with a shiny white shell called mother-of-pearl. The Franciscans may have directed native artisans to make an altarpiece at Mission Santa Bárbara featuring a mother-of-pearl crucifix and abalone shell.

Some mission Indians used their artistic skills to paint walls and ceilings with bright borders and geometric designs. Sometimes the paints came on

The central coast missions contain portraits, borders, sculptures, and carvings done by neophyte artists.

supply ships from New Spain. But the neophytes often made the paints themselves by grinding up clay, minerals, water, and cactus juice. (The juice helped bind the mixture together.) Other Chumash recruited to the missions carved statues and water spouts out of local stone.

Adobe, a readily available clay, became the preferred building material at the missions. The Indians blended the clay with straw and water to form a thick, sticky mixture. They then poured the mixture into rectangular molds and left them in the sun to dry. The dried bricks, layered with limestone mortar, were set within wooden frames to make walls. Clay could also be shaped into curved tiles for roofing.

The increasingly restless soldiers at the mission treated the Indians cruelly. At the same time, a large comet appeared in the sky and developed twin tails. For the Chumash, the unusual sighting meant sudden change and new beginnings.

The change came in the form of the revolt of February 1824, which began at Mission Santa Inés and spread to the other two missions. A neophyte named Pacomio led the rebellion at La Purísima. Outnumbering the soldiers, the neophytes forced the priests and soldiers into a storeroom and quickly gained

*During the 1824 rebellion at La Purísima, neophytes raised a barricade in front of the church and were able to occupy the mission for a month before heavily armed Spanish soldiers defeated them.*

*After the revolt, La Purísima quickly fell into ruin. Within a few decades, the interior of the church was sorely in need of repair.*

control of the mission. The Indians then built a defensive wall and mounted cannons in front of the church. The rebels held La Purísima for about a month.

Using their heaviest weapons, soldiers eventually put down the revolt. In a battle that lasted for three hours, 16 Native Americans were killed, and many were wounded. One of the soldiers died, and three others were injured.

After the conflict ended, seven Indians received a death sentence, and many went to prison. Over time La Purísima continued

The spot chosen as the site for Mission Santa Inés lay in the foothills of the Santa Ynez Mountains.

to decline. Indians fled the mission, which slowly decayed and fell into ruin.

# Mission Santa Inés

The brand for Santa Inés twists together the letters S and I. The mission's name honors Saint Agnes, who in the early fourth century A.D. was executed in Italy for following the Christian religion.

By the early 1800s, 18 missions had been established in Alta California. The missions were producing a wealth of goods such as hides, wines, fruits, and vegetables. At the missions, the priests had baptized thousands of Native Americans.

The Franciscans wanted to found another mission in the central coast region. The chosen site, sheltered by the Santa Ynez Mountains, lay midway between Santa Bárbara and La Purísima. Here stood the villages of approximately 1,000 inland Chumash. The Santa Ynez River would provide water for drinking, for washing, and for irrigating crops.

On September 17, 1804, the nineteenth mission—Santa Inés Virgen y Mártir—was founded in the Santa Ynez Valley. Father Estéban Tápis, the father-president at that time, planted a cross and blessed the settlement. Neophytes arrived from neighboring missions to help construct buildings.

But few inland Chumash were interested in joining this new settlement. Most of the nearby Native Americans remained in their villages and lived as they always had. In the first year after the mission's

*The Franciscans color-coded music for the church choir. Singers were instructed to sound only their assigned notes.*

*The Santa Ynez River watered the fertile fields of Mission Santa Inés.*

founding, the priests didn't have enough Indian workers for the mission to succeed. As a result, Franciscans at the other two central coast missions sent a total of nearly 300 neophytes to live at Santa Inés.

The fertile soils around the mission provided excellent ground for planting crops and for grazing cattle. In fact, the mission became known for its high crop yields and large herds. During its best years, Santa Inés supported about 13,000 farm animals on its lush grazing lands. Fields of barley, corn, and beans flourished.

*Among the buildings raised by the neophyte labor force was the arcade that held the priests' quarters. The arched walkway was connected to the church, which formed one corner of the four-sided quadrangle.*

*The church's heavy wooden door features a wavy carving known as the "river of life."*

Neophytes at the mission took about one year to build the adobe church at Santa Inés. Father José Antonio Calzada, the priest in charge of the mission for the next 10 years, supervised this project and many others. Along the mission's growing quadrangle sat workshops, storerooms, and the priests' quarters.

At the workshops, Chumash neophytes were taught to produce a wide variety of goods that helped the mission to prosper. The Indians made soap, spun wool, and fashioned iron tools. People far and wide knew of the mission's fine leatherwork, especially its saddles.

# Trouble at the Mission

The earthquake of December 1812 also struck a terrible blow to Mission Santa Inés, destroying the church and damaging other buildings. Over the next few years, the neophytes were busy constructing a new church. Its walls stood six feet thick to prevent future damage to the structure.

In 1818 a pirate named Hippolyte de Bouchard raided Alta California and looted missions and presidios. Fearing loss of life and church valuables, the people of Santa Inés fled into the hills. They buried the mission's treasures and waited for the pirate ship to leave the coast.

*After an earthquake tumbled the church in 1812, neophytes built a new, thick-walled structure (right). The remains of an original archway are on display at the mission (inset).*

# Joseph Chapman, the Yankee at Santa Inés

Among the people on board the pirate ship of Hippolyte de Bouchard was a young U.S. citizen named Joseph Chapman. He wasn't exactly a pirate, for he'd been kidnapped and added to the crew against his will.

As the raiding party came down the coast of California in 1818, Chapman saw his chance to escape. Under cover of darkness, he made his way over the Santa Ynez Mountains to Mission Santa Inés. He told his tale to the mission's priests, who agreed to give him protection.

Eventually, Chapman settled in the Santa Ynez Valley. His talents at making and repairing anything, from stone walls to artworks, made him a favorite at Santa Inés. In fact, he used his skills to build a gristmill—one of the first in the mission chain. This device crushed grain into flour, using animals as the power source.

In 1822 Chapman married the daughter of a local rancher. He became a well-known citizen and was buried in the cemetery at Santa Bárbara. Long after his death, the historian Hubert Howe Bancroft wrote of Chapman, "Among all the earliest pioneers of California there was no more attractive character, no more popular and useful man, than Joseph Chapman, the Yankee."

*Sections of the gristmill still stand at Santa Inés.*

As it turned out, the mission was unharmed. To protect themselves from possible attack in the future, the missionaries armed and organized the neophytes.

During these troubling times, Mission Santa Inés continued to prosper economically. It produced enough goods to support its own people and to trade with other settlements. This success wouldn't have been possible without the hard work of the neophytes.

Most of the inland Chumash who eventually came to Mission

*Many of the inland Chumash who made up Santa Inés's workforce wanted to return to the old ways of hunting, gathering, and providing food for their families.*

*Clashes between Spanish soldiers and neophytes sparked the 1824 revolt that began at Santa Inés.*

Santa Inés had had little previous contact with the Spaniards. Mission settlements restricted their customs and made it nearly impossible to live traditionally. Upon joining the mission, these Native Americans had to adjust to new routines of Catholic prayer and mission work. Many of the Indians disliked the new regimens and longed for the old ways of hunting and gathering to support their families.

In 1824 a Spanish soldier whipped a neophyte who was visiting Santa Inés from La Purísima. The soldier's action sparked other neophytes to fight back with their bows and arrows. Two Indians died in the conflict. Fires soon started at the mission, destroying part of the church. The next day, soldiers from Santa Bárbara arrived, and some of the Indians escaped to La Purísima, where the fighting continued.

After the conflict spread to La Purísima and Santa Bárbara, the three central coast missions went into decline. But harder times were yet to come.

When the revolt started at Santa Inés in 1824, some neophytes firmly believed that a shaman's power could outlast the soldiers' weapons and the priests' religion. They were convinced that the Spaniards' guns couldn't wound Indians. One shaman declared, "The priests cannot hurt me . . . . If they shoot at me water will come out of the cannon, [and] the bullet will not enter my flesh."

# PART THREE

# *Secularization of the Missions*

AROUND THE TIME THAT THE NEOPHYTES OF THE central coast revolted, changes had been taking place in Alta California. In 1821 New Spain won its independence from Spain to become the Republic of Mexico. Afterward Mexican officials invited Mexican soldiers and settlers into Alta California to claim the land. The invitation was partly inspired by a fear that other countries might try to seize control of the region.

In years past, Spain had forbidden the missions from trading with anyone but Spain. Spanish supply ships often failed to arrive, however, and many missionaries felt they had no choice but to barter

*A nineteenth-century illustration shows the expanding town and port of Santa Barbara.*

for goods with foreigners. The new Mexican government resented the presence of traders from the United States, Britain, and France. But seafarers still sailed into the Santa Barbara Channel, and some eventually settled near the missions to live as merchants or ranchers. Fur trappers and mountaineers also found their way westward across the Rocky Mountains and into the region.

At the central coast missions, the traders received cattle hides, tallow, wine, and crops in exchange for books, tools, or religious items that interested the priests. The foreigners later returned home, bringing stories of the fabulous wealth of the Spanish missions.

*By the early 1820s, neophyte laborers were producing a wealth of everyday goods, including rope, that supplied the missions and were also bartered for other necessities.*

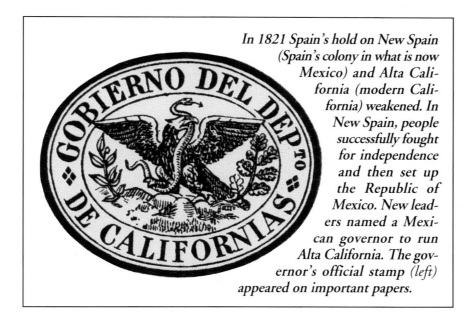

In 1821 Spain's hold on New Spain (Spain's colony in what is now Mexico) and Alta California (modern California) weakened. In New Spain, people successfully fought for independence and then set up the Republic of Mexico. New leaders named a Mexican governor to run Alta California. The governor's official stamp (left) appeared on important papers.

To address the growing risk of foreign settlement, Mexican officials tried to convince more and more Mexicans to move to Alta California. But farming and ranching the region would be too difficult, the people in Mexico argued, because the Franciscan priests controlled the best land.

Meanwhile, in Alta California, Californios (settlers of Spanish descent) were jealous of the missions' rich property and vast supply of unpaid neophyte laborers. Wanting successful ranches and farms of their own, the Californios complained to the Mexican government that the missions held too much power in Alta California.

In the 1830s, to end the mission system, the Mexican government began to pass laws that would take mission lands and property away from the Franciscans. This policy was known as secularization. Mission fields, pastures, and herds would be redistributed among ex-neophytes, Californios, and other settlers. Officials ruled that the missions would be run by secular priests—men who wouldn't try to convert people to the Catholic faith.

The Mexican government hoped that by providing the Indians with land, tools, and farm animals, the ex-neophytes could survive on their own and would be less likely to rebel. Mexico reasoned that secularization would finally accomplish the original goal of the missions—to make the Indians self-sufficient citizens.

During secularization the government turned the mission lands and buildings over to civil administrators. These overseers were told to divide the properties fairly among the Indians, the Californios, and non-Spanish

settlers. But some administrators had other ideas. Many were greedy and saw secularization as an opportunity to gain wealth.

Although some neophytes received supplies, few got the land that had been promised to them. Instead, the administra-

tors took the land for their own families and friends. Those ex-neophytes who did receive some acreage often lost it. Californios

*Secularization laws passed by Mexico in the 1830s removed mission estates from Franciscan control. La Purísima's herds and farmland (above) were sold to private owners who used the old priests' quarters as a stable. Mexican settlers looked over the fertile land around Mission Santa Bárbara (left).*

*On Mexican-owned ranches in California, vaqueros, or cowboys (left), herded cattle on horseback. Some ex-neophytes got jobs on the ranches for little or no pay. This worker (below) was called a zanjero and had the task of clearing irrigation ditches.*

tricked the Indians, who weren't familiar with laws of landownership. As a result, many of the Indians were left without any property at all.

Lacking adequate shelter and the means to make their own living among the settlers, many Indians ended up working on ranchos owned by Californios. These Native American laborers were given little more than room and board. Some Native Americans fled the area, heading inland to join other Indian communities.

## Secularization along the Central Coast

In 1834 all three missions of the central coast were secularized. At Santa Bárbara, the missionaries were left with only their living quarters, the church, and the cemetery. The civil administrator divided up the remaining property, which went mainly to Californios.

Father Narciso Durán, who was father-president of the missions at this time, lived at Santa Bárbara. Opposed to secularization, he argued with Mexican officials and tried to prevent the Indians from being treated unfairly. But he accomplished little in the face of so many changes. By 1839 only 246 Indians were left at the mission.

Secularization also hit La Purísima hard. The civil administrators stole mission property and mistreated the Indians.

Within six months, La Purísima had lost half its wealth. By 1836 the church had collapsed. Only 200 Indians were living at the mission by 1844. Not long afterward, a smallpox epidemic wiped out the remaining Native Americans.

At Santa Inés, a secular priest was in charge of the mission church by 1834. Two years later, the governor rented other mission buildings to José Covarrubias and his family. The priests lived at the church, where they built a

*Father Narciso Durán, who was opposed to secularization, lived at Santa Bárbara and listened to the concerns of ex-neophytes after the mission lands were given away. By the late 1830s, most Indians had left the mission.*

*At Santa Inés, a rough stone wall separated the priests' quarters from former mission property, which had been rented to a Mexican family.*

wall to separate themselves from the Covarrubias family. During this time, the remaining ex-neophytes left the mission.

In 1842 Santa Bárbara became the headquarters of García Diego y Moreno, Alta California's first bishop (high-ranking church official). The next year, he established a seminary (school for training new priests) at nearby Santa Inés. The bishop remained at Santa Bárbara for the rest of his life. He died in 1846, just a month before fellow

*A gathering of priests, settlers, and ex-neophytes welcomed Bishop García Diego y Moreno to Santa Bárbara in 1842.*

resident Father Durán also passed away.

Soon after these events, Pío Pico, one of the last Mexican governors of California, sold Mission Santa Bárbara. Governor

> PÍO PICO, ONE OF CALIFORNIA'S LAST MEXICAN GOVERNORS, OPENLY DECLARED, "I WAS DETERMINED TO PUT AN END TO THE MISSION SYSTEM . . . IN ORDER THAT THE LAND COULD BE ACQUIRED BY PRIVATE INDIVIDUALS."

Pico had been bent on doing away with the missions and intended to grant the lands to private individuals. But before the new owner could take over the property at Santa Bárbara, Mexico began to lose control of Alta California to the United States.

## War and Statehood

Border disputes between Mexico and the United States had bred tension for a number of years. By the summer of 1846, the two countries were at war. Determined to take control of Alta California, the U.S. Navy successfully landed at Monterey.

Few battles of the war actually took place in Alta California, however. When the conflict ended in 1848, the United States had officially gained control of the region. In 1850 the U.S. government made California, as it became known, the thirty-first state.

People entered the new state in droves. Gold seekers arrived to find their fortunes, and California's mining industry boomed. Settlers came from the eastern United States and from Europe and Asia in search of wealth and farmland. Many of these newcomers claimed the right to farm and raise cattle on territory occupied by Indians or Californios.

In the central coast region and throughout California, costly court battles over

*Pío Pico*

landownership occurred. Many Californios couldn't afford legal trials and lost their land. Native Americans usually fared much worse. Settlers pushed them off their land. Native Americans had no legal rights under federal

(Above) Mexico and the United States clashed in the Mexican War (1846–1848). Americans cheered the raising of the U.S. flag at the Presidio of Monterey (a military outpost in Alta California). Postwar agreements gave the territory to the United States. (Right) Within a year, gold had been discovered and drew people to the region from the eastern United States.

By the 1830s, only 20 Indians were still living on San Nicolas Island. In 1835 the priests at Santa Bárbara decided to remove the last residents. A boat crossed the sea to collect them. One of the Indian women realized her baby hadn't been brought on board, and she dove off the departing vessel to swim for shore. During the next 18 years, people made several rescue attempts, but neither the woman nor her child were found.

In 1853 Captain George Nidever and his crew solved the mystery. On the island, they found footprints, a brush shelter, and, at last, the missing woman. She made them understand that her child was dead and that she was all alone. The crew brought her to the mainland, where she was baptized Juana Maria. But Juana Maria had trouble adjusting to her new environment and died within seven weeks of her arrival. She's buried at Mission Santa Bárbara.

or state laws and could not testify against whites in court. As a result, the Indians had to fight these wrongs on their own.

By the late 1800s, the U.S. government was sending Indians to **reservations.** On these tracts of land, Native Americans lived apart from the non-native population. But few Indians could support their families on the reservations because the land lacked water and was difficult to farm. The people became dependent on government-supplied food and other necessities, which were often slow in coming. Many Native Americans in

*(Above left) Mexican families living in California used the carreta as a means of traveling from place to place. (Left) In the mid-1800s, the U.S. government began relocating Indians to reservations, which often relied on outside food supplies. Some Chumash were sent to the Santa Ynez Reservation, near Mission Santa Inés.*

*By the late 1800s, the church and arcade at Santa Inés (above) and the walkway at La Purísima (inset) were showing signs of decay.*

California died from poverty and disease. One of the reservations lay along Zanja de Cota Creek near Mission Santa Inés. In 1855 about 100 Chumash moved to this 120-acre territory, which became the state's smallest Indian reservation.

Meanwhile, the U.S. government had returned the missions to the Catholic Church. Most of the settlements had been robbed, neglected, and then abandoned. By the late 1880s, many of the buildings were in ruins, and the Church lacked the funds to repair the collapsed roofs and the rotted walls.

# PART FOUR

# The Missions in Modern Times

CALIFORNIA'S RUINED MISSIONS DIDN'T ATTRACT much attention until the late 1800s. At that time, the U.S. government appointed Helen Hunt Jackson, a talented writer, to report on the Indians of California. She toured the missions and ranchos and later described how the buildings had fallen apart. "The most desolate ruin of all is that of La Purísima Mission. Nothing is left but one long, low adobe building, with a few arches of the corridor; the door stands wide open, the roof is falling in . . . ."

*The British painter Edwin Deakin recorded the crumbling condition of each of the 21 missions, including La Purísima, in the early 1900s.*

*Through her writings, Helen Hunt Jackson (above) criticized the U.S. government for its treatment of Native Americans in California. A Chumash couple (right) posed outside Mission Santa Bárbara in the early twentieth century.*

But Jackson was even more upset about the way the Indians in California had been treated. In her view, their lands had been unfairly taken by U.S. settlers. When the government did nothing to fix the problem, Jackson herself addressed it by writing a novel. Published in 1884, *Ramona* showed people the conditions under which Native Americans lived. But instead of moving people to act on the abuses, the story inspired readers across the nation to view the historic missions in a romantic light.

The public's interest in mission history eventually led to the formation of organizations such as the Landmarks Club. This group and others like it raised money to repair the ruined missions. Officials and businesspeople in the state supported the rebuilding because the sites would draw tourists—and tourists' dollars—to California.

## Santa Bárbara

Mission Santa Bárbara never fell into decay as most other missions did. It served as a religious school for a number of years, and the Catholic Church kept the buildings in good repair. But in 1925, a huge earthquake struck the central coast region.

As the church swayed from side to side, statues in the altar toppled from their bases. One of the bell towers crumbled, and

the other one cracked and lost its dome. The walls of the priests' living quarters caved in. One priest survived a fall through a hole created on the second floor of the building. After the earthquake, citizens donated $400,000 toward the restoration of Mission Santa Bárbara.

But by 1950, the rebuilt towers had begun to crack because the cement was crumbling. As a result, workers tore down and completely restored the facade and bell towers to their original appearance. Workers finished the job in 1953.

The many visitors who come to the mission appreciate its architectural beauty and its famous museum, archive, and library. Within the archive are detailed records of the Chumash who once inhabited the region. The library houses old mission documents and rare books from the early days of Spanish settlement. Fine religious paintings and sculptures decorate the

*Mission Santa Bárbara (above) was in fairly good shape until an earthquake heavily damaged it in 1925. Repeated restoration efforts reconstructed the mission's towers and facade (below).*

# I Madonnari

Each year thousands of people gather in front of Mission Santa Bárbara to celebrate I Madonnari, a street-painting festival patterned after a centuries-old Italian event. Beginning in the 1500s, Italian artists traveled from town to town attending religious festivals. In front of every Catholic church they passed, the illustrators created complex chalk images of Mary, the mother of Jesus. Because Mary is also called the Madonna, the artists came to be known as I Madonnari (the Madonnaists).

The present-day Madonnari make traditional religious drawings, reproduce famous artworks, or create original works. The illustrations stretch outward in marked-off rectangles from the church's facade (front).

The festival of I Madonnari draws people to Mission Santa Bárbara in May.

church. Tourists stroll the mission grounds and the complex system that once carried water to the settlement. People also visit the walled, shaded Indian cemetery where more than 4,000 neophytes are buried.

## Santa Inés

Father Alexander Buckler worked to rebuild parts of Mission Santa Inés from 1904 to 1924. Heavy rains in 1911 knocked down the adobe *campanario* (bell wall). Buckler replaced it with a concrete, plaster, and wood structure that lasted until 1948.

The priest's niece, Mamie Goulet, traveled from her home in Minnesota to assist in the restoration of the mission. She helped repair and restore the old religious garments that the Franciscans had once worn. Goulet stayed at Santa Inés until her uncle's death in 1930. Further restoration on the mission buildings took place from 1953 to 1954.

Mission Santa Inés is a parish church. Nestled in a lush valley near the little town of Solvang, the church also serves as a hub of community activity. Visitors can view the original mission bells. The foundation and buildings of the old gristmill that Joseph Chapman had set up in the early 1800s are also on display.

*In the early 1900s, repairs of the roof and arches at Santa Inés (above) were guided by Father Alexander Buckler (inset, on ladder). The mission's chapel (left) serves a small Catholic congregation in Solvang, California.*

# La Purísima

Although a pile of rubble before restoration, La Purísima looks as it did long ago. The rebuilt mission, which sits just east of the city of Lompoc, draws visitors from around the world. Many experts regard the mission as the most authentic restoration of a historic site in the western United States.

Workers hired by a U.S. government agency called the Civilian Conservation Corps began rebuilding the mission in 1934. They labored under the direction of two archaeologists—Arthur Woodward and M. R. Harrington. Other restorers included Harry Downie and Edith Webb, famous for their contributions to preserving mission history. From 1935 to 1937, the workers rebuilt the priests' living quarters. Workshops, neophyte housing, warehouses, and

*(Left) La Purísima's restoration became a project of the Civilian Conservation Corps in the 1930s. (Above) As part of La Purísima's living history program, volunteers show how pottery was made during the mission period.*

# A Lesson in Soapmaking

The restoration of La Purísima includes a "living history" program in which trained volunteers act out aspects of daily life. One of the demonstrations is of soapmaking.

The volunteer first cooks pieces of beef fat to collect its tallow. Production of lye, a strong chemical also known as sodium hydroxide (NaOH), comes next. To make lye, the soapmaker pours water through a box of ashes—which naturally contain NaOH—until the liquid absorbs the chemical. The volunteer then mixes the liquid with the tallow in a pot over an open fire.

When the tallow-and-lye mixture reaches the right temperature, it is poured into molds, allowed to cool, and cut into cakes of soap. Visitors at La Purísima can buy the soap in the mission's gift shop.

the cemetery also underwent reconstruction.

The laborers made adobe bricks and clay roof tiles by hand, just as the neophytes had done long ago. The restorers also furnished rooms throughout the mission and strengthened walls to prevent earthquake damage. The large mission church was finished and rededicated in 1941. The restoration took 200 workers about seven years to complete. Even the mission gardens—filled with the kinds of herbs, fruits, and vegetables once used by the Franciscans— are now true to history.

Paying a visit to La Purísima is like stepping into the past. Volunteers in historic clothing follow the routines of 1820s mission life. Robed priests stroll the arched corridors, while uniformed soldiers play cards in their quarters. Expert weavers spin yarn on the mission's looms. Neophytes dip candles in kettles and cook bread in outdoor ovens.

*Docents (guides) dress in mission-era clothing at La Purísima and explain the use of artifacts to visitors.*

Beyond the valleys and mountain foothills that sheltered the missions of the central coast are the trees and hills where Chumash villages once flourished. Surviving descendants of mission Chumash chose to live on the reservation near Zanja de Cota Creek. Here, they could practice some traditional ways and set up their own governmental system.

The reservation is still an active hub of Chumash culture. Its

*Much of what historians know about Chumash lifeways came from the writings, reports, and demonstrations of a Chumash named Kitsepawit (pictured above), whom the Franciscans named Fernando Librado.*

*Modern Chumash continue to preserve their culture through gatherings at which people wear traditional clothing (right) or learn new skills (far right).*

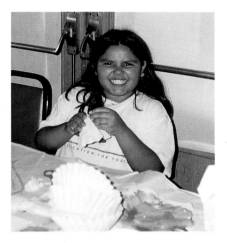

residents hold festivals and other gatherings at various times of the year to share with young Chumash—as well as with other people—the age-old dances, foods, and crafts. To further keep their culture alive, Chumash in the central coast area visit schools to talk about the people's way of life and their relationship to the environment. Still other members participate in cultural societies that strive to preserve sacred and historic places throughout the lands that once were home to large Chumash communities.

Bathed in sunlight, the missions of the central coast still overlook the sea. In the distance lay the offshore islands, washed by the endless rhythm of the tides.

*Crops such as Swiss chard thrive on the lands that once were inhabited by thousands of Chumash and later were planted under the direction of the missionaries.*

73

# AFTERWORD

Each year thousands of tourists and students visit the California missions. Many of these visitors look around and conclude that the missions are the same today as they were long ago. But, over time, the missions have gone through many changes. The earliest structures were replaced by sturdier buildings with tall towers and long arcades. But even these solid buildings eventually fell into ruin and later were reconstructed.

Our understanding of the missions also has changed through the years. Missionaries, visitors, novelists, and scholars have expressed different opinions about the California missions. These observers often have disagreed about the impact of the missions on the Indians in California. And the voices of Native Americans—from the past *and* the present—have continued to shed light on the mission experience.

The early Franciscan missionaries believed that they were improving the local Indians by introducing them to mission life. But visitors from Europe and the United States frequently described the Spanish missions as cruel places. A French explorer in 1786, for example, reported that the priests treated the neophytes like slaves. He was horrified that Spanish soldiers tracked down runaway Indians and whipped them for trying to return to their old way of life.

Many early visitors were truly concerned about the mistreatment of Native Americans. But the foreign travelers, jealous of Spain's hold on Alta California, also criticized the missions as a way to prove that Spain wasn't worthy to possess the region. Similarly, a young man from the eastern United States, visiting Alta California in the 1830s, was saddened to see so much sickness and death at the missions. He advised his fellow Americans that the region would fare much better as a part of the United States.

The missions were all but forgotten during the 25 years following the U.S. takeover of California. The once solid structures decayed into piles of rotting adobe. One U.S. visitor wrote that she doubted if any structure on earth was "colder, barer, uglier, [or] dirtier" than a California mission.

Just when the missions had disappeared almost completely, they came roaring back to public attention. Beginning in the 1880s, dozens of novels and plays about early California described the Franciscan priests as kind-hearted souls who treated neophytes with gentleness and care. This favorable image of the missions became popular because it gave many Californians a positive sense of their own history and identity. The writings also attracted droves of tourists to California. Merchants and business leaders in the state supported the rebuilding of the crumbling missions because it made good business sense.

The missions today are still the subject of a lively debate. Some people continue to believe that the missions brought many benefits to the Indians by "uplifting" them to European ways. But many others, including some descendants of the neophytes, say that the missions destroyed Native American lifeways and killed thousands of Indians. For all of us, the missions continue to stand as reminders of a difficult and painful time in California history.

*Dr. James J. Rawls*
Diablo Valley College

# CHRONOLOGY

*Important Dates in the History of the Missions of the Central Coast*

| | |
|---|---|
| **1542** | Juan Rodríguez Cabrillo sails along the central coast |
| **1602** | Sebastián Vizcaíno repeats Cabrillo's route and names the area Santa Barbara |
| **1769** | San Diego de Alcalá, the first Franciscan mission in Alta California, is founded |
| **1782** | Soldiers begin building a presidio at Santa Barbara |
| **1784** | Father Junípero Serra dies; Father Fermín Francisco de Lasuén becomes the new father-president |
| **1786** | Mission Santa Bárbara Virgen y Mártir is founded |
| **1787** | Father Lasuén sets up Mission La Purísima Concepción de Maria Santísima |
| **1804** | Mission Santa Inés Virgen y Mártir is established |
| **1821** | New Spain gains independence from Spain |
| **1824** | Indian revolts spread through the central coast missions |
| **1830s** | Missions are secularized |
| **1846** | Mexican War begins; U.S. Navy occupies Monterey |
| **1848** | Mexican War ends; Mexico cedes Alta California to the United States |
| **1850** | California becomes the thirty-first state |
| **1850s** | U.S. government begins to return the California missions to the Catholic Church; mission buildings are falling apart |
| **1890s– present** | Missions are restored |

# ACKNOWLEDGMENTS

Photos, maps, and artworks are used courtesy of: Laura Westlund, pp. 1, 13, 19, 28 (bottom), 29, 36, 44 (bottom); © Diane C. Lyell, pp. 2, 69 (top); Southwest Museum, Los Angeles, CA, pp. 8-9 (photo by Don Meyer, CT. 374-646.G136), 22 (left); North Wind Picture Archives, pp. 10, 43, 54, 62 (top); © Betty Crowell, pp. 12, 15, 44 (top), 73 (top left and bottom); © Carol Stiver, pp. 16, 31, 38 (left); © Jo-Ann Ordano, pp. 16 (bottom inset), 18 (inset), ; © Richard R. Hansen, pp. 16 (top inset), 18 (top right), 49; © Frank S. Balthis, pp. 18 (top left), 38 (right), 46 (left), 72 (left); © Reno A. DiTullio, pp. 18 (bottom), 48; Coll. of the Santa Barbara Hist. Soc., pp. 20 (top), 24, 30; © Shirley Jordan, pp. 20 (bottom), 38 (bottom left), 39, 48 (inset); Santa Barbara Mus. of Nat. Hist., pp. 66 (right), 72 (right); IPS, pp. 23, 28 (top), 32 (right), 34, 35, 40 (right), 45, 51, 55, 56 (bottom), 57 (right), 58, 59 (bottom), 61 (left), 63 (inset), 67 (top), 69 (inset); © Chuck Place, pp. 26, 32 (left), 42, 46 (right), 47, 67 (bottom), 68; June Behrens, pp. 33, 80 (top); David Rucker, p. 39; © D. J. Lambrecht, pp. 41, 69 (bottom); © Eda Rogers, pp. 22 (right), 50, 59 (top). 70 (right), 71; Historic Urban Plans, p. 52; Bancroft Lib., pp. 56 (top), 57 (left), 62 (bottom); The Huntington Lib., p. 60; Nat'l Cowboy Hall of Fame and Western Heritage Center, Oklahoma City, p. 61 (right); CA Hist. Society/Ticor Coll., USC, p. 63; Seaver Center for Western History Research, Nat. Hist. Mus. of Los Angeles Cty., p. 64; Library of Congress, p. 66 (left); La Purísima Mission State Historic Park, p. 70 (left); Santa Ynez Reservation, p. 73 (top right); IPS/photo by Nancy Smedstad, pp. 74-75; Dr. James J. Rawls, p. 80 (middle); Professor Edward D. Castillo, p. 80 (bottom). Cover (Front) © Chuck Place; (Back) Laura Westlund.

Quotations are from the original or translated writings or statements of a member of the Cabrillo expedition (as recorded by H. E. Bolton), p. 25; Father Antonio Ripoll, pp. 35, 37 (with Father Mariano Payeras); Hubert Howe Bancroft, pp. 40, 49; Governor Pío Pico, p. 60; Helen Hunt Jackson, p. 65.

## METRIC CONVERSION CHART

| WHEN YOU KNOW | MULTIPLY BY | TO FIND |
|---|---|---|
| inches | 2.54 | centimeters |
| feet | 0.3048 | meters |
| miles | 1.609 | kilometers |
| square feet | 0.0929 | square meters |
| acres | 0.4047 | hectares |
| ounces | 28.3495 | grams |
| pounds | 0.454 | kilograms |
| gallons | 3.7854 | liters |

# INDEX